How to Improve Your Public Speaking

Seven Basic Techniques You Need to Win the Audience

Neal Hoffman

Legal & Disclaimer

The information contained in this book is not designed to replace or take the place of any form of medicine or professional medical advice. The information in this book has been provided for educational and entertainment purposes only.

The information contained in this book has been compiled from sources deemed reliable, and it is accurate to the best of the Author's knowledge; however, the Author cannot guarantee its accuracy and validity and cannot be held liable for any errors or omissions. Changes are periodically made to this book. You must consult your doctor or get professional medical advice before using any of the suggested remedies, techniques, or information in this book.

Upon using the information contained in this book, you agree to hold harmless the Author from and against any damages, costs, and expenses, including any legal fees potentially resulting from the application of any of the information provided by this guide. This disclaimer applies to any damages or injury caused by the use and application, whether directly or indirectly, of any advice or information presented, whether for breach of contract, tort, negligence, personal injury, criminal intent, or under any other cause of action.

You agree to accept all risks of using the information presented inside this book. You need to consult a professional medical practitioner in order to ensure you are both able and healthy enough to participate in this program.

Table of Contents

Introduction

Public speaking is something many of us have to do in our daily lives, whether it's in the educational system or our occupation. It's a way to connect with an audience on their level and convey a message to them that truly means something to the speaker and them, but what do you do if you're not able to speak publically with etiquette and poise?

Stage fright, being underprepared, not knowing how to capture an audience, poor body language, and having a boring speech are all complications public speakers go through. Even a person who gets up on the stage regularly still has to contend with some or even all of the aforementioned obstacles. Public speaking is not easy, even if you're someone who is at ease with the notion. Being someone who experiences stage fright and panic attacks before a speech makes it just *that* much more difficult to get through the experience.

So how can you move past these obstacles?

In this book, I'm going to teach you how to create the ultimate speech before you even step up to the podium. You're going to learn how to be the best speech writer there is, and then I'm going to teach you how to overcome the anxiety holding you back by giving you tips on how to move past anxiety, fear, and desperation before you walk up to the podium, even *as* you're walking up to the podium.

Then you're going to learn how to compose your body so your physical language is engaging the audience rather than turning them away. Most of us don't realize how much our body language affects the everyday conversations we have, let alone the important ones that change our lives.

If you want to learn how to take control of your thoughts, emotions, and grab the audience with a speech so compelling they'll be talking about it for days after you've stopped talking, then keep reading this book!

Chapter One - Creating the Ultimate Public Speech

Let's face it, you can be the best speech giver out there and still have a dud of a speech, so how do you create one that's going to grab your audience and really engage them in what you're trying to convey? Follow these six steps and you'll be on your way to having the ultimate public speech, all you'll need afterward is the ability to express it properly!

Step One – Select Your Topic

It seems like the easiest task out of everything, and it may have already been selected for you if you're doing this for educational purposes, but the speech topic is imperative to your success. There are an infinite number of topics available to you when it comes to public speaking, so how do you choose the one that will wow the audience and one you can stand behind?

Your topic is your core message. The presentation is going to aim to deliver this core message to the audience. Before you choose your topic, you want to figure out what type of speech you're delivering.

The three different types are as follows:

- Educational: This speech will educate the audience on a subject, such as real estate investments.

- Motivational: These speeches aim to get the audience to take action when it comes to something particular, such as a fundraiser.

- Entertainment: Speeches that will entertain the audience, such as an after-dinner speech or a wedding toast.

Once you know what type of speech you're delivering, you need to analyze your audience by answering these key questions:

- What is the demographic of the audience? Are they students, parents, business leaders, predominately men or women, non-technical or tech savvy, elderly, etc.

- How do they relate to you? Is the audience your peers, superiors, or subordinates and do they relate to you or are you viewed as an expert?

- How large is your audience? Is it so small everyone will see your face starting to sweat or is it in a large theater?

- What message does your audience want to obtain? This is just as important as being passionate because if you're passionate and your audience doesn't care about the subject at hand, they will still tune out.

Once you know your audience and what they're looking for, you'll still need to figure out the scope of the presentation. The scope is going to be influenced by the aforementioned points. It's these three things combined:

- The general purpose

- The core message

- The needs of the audience

But there is one more thing you must consider, what are the constraints on the speech?

- How much time has been allotted for the speech? If you have two minutes, then you want to tell one story to illustrate your message. If you have four hours, you might want to talk about many different avenues of your topic.

- What is the context? Are there going to be others who are speaking about the same subject, opposing viewpoints, or will it just be you talking about the subject? This determines how deep you're going to travel into the subject. If others are talking about it, you want to keep your context narrow so as to focus on one aspect. If there will be no one else talking about it, then you'll want to make your subject broad.

Once you know all of those things, then you can choose a topic that will fit both you and your audience.

Step Two – Make a Speech Outline

Your speech is going to need structure, without it, the audience is going to wonder what the core message is or they're going to lose interest.

An outline of a presentation is going to highlight key elements that support the core message, highlight structural elements like the introduction, body, and conclusion, and link the elements together in a sequential order so it makes sense. There will also be transitions between each element. A basic outline is as such:

- Introduction: This is where you introduce the core message and topic.

- Body: This is where the supporting points will be listed.

    o Supporting Point One

    o Two

    o Three

- Conclusion: This is going to recap those main points and give the audience a call to action, if necessary.

Some other key points to remember while you're creating your outline are:

- Each point on the outline should equate to about one minute, two at the most, of speaking time. This way the audience stays engaged and is not bored.

- The outline can include presentation slides, but only put slide concepts up there and not fine points, those are just a guideline.

- Remember the presentation is more than just the slides. The outline is what you should focus on; the slides will come after, not before.

- When sequencing outline points, avoid random order. Find the meaningful relationship between points.

- The outline is not your cue cards, but the two are related. An outline is going to contain the high-level element and the cue cards are going to contain speech details, too.

Creating an outline should be done with the core audience in mind.

Step Three – Write Your Speech

Writing the speech is actually one of the most difficult parts of the process. What are you going to say? How are you going to say it? And is it going to be interesting enough? Those are the questions we all battle with on a daily basis, whether you're writing or talking.

One of the most common problems people come across as they begin to write is they don't know what to write. It's a very common cause of writer's block. Another cause is having a large ego. Most believe their first draft has to be perfect and if it's not, they're going to fail. Well, the first draft is called the *first* one for a reason. Go back and edit it to make it better when you're finished writing it. You'll feel a lot more accomplished at that point.

Some other key points to keep in mind while you're writing are:

- Set a deadline so you create a draft in a single sitting.

- Write in bullet form if you can't think of any sentences. Getting the ideas down on paper, or on the computer, is what matters.

- Write out of sequence. You don't have to write the introduction before you finish the conclusion. If you know what you're going to say in the conclusion, write it. Then go back and fill in the other parts.

- Don't worry about the transitions. Just put in notations where you need them and move on. You can fill those in on the second draft.

- Don't worry about the wording. Just get the ideas down using whatever words come to mind. Words can easily be changed in the second or third draft.

- Don't worry about the length. It's okay if it's too long or too short, this can be solved in editing.

- Don't use too many details. A good first draft is going to contain ideas and quotes from sources, not much else.

- Don't be bogged down with technology. If you're comfortable with a pen and some paper, go for it!

- Don't worry about colors, font sizes, drawings, or design criteria on your slides just yet.

- Slides are not your first draft. Produce a short first draft on the oral part of the speech and then make your slides.

Remember your speech should be written for the audience, so keep how it's going to sound in mind. If you have a lot of words ending and beginning with the same letters and they might run together, find synonyms. Talk out loud as you write the first draft to figure out what you can change.

Step Four – Editing

There are two different forms of editing a speech. There's macro-editing, which involves looking to make sure paragraphs, sections, transitions, and stories are all organized into a speech that will deliver the core message. Then there's micro-editing, which ensures sentences, phrases, and words will all invoke emotion and make images last with the audience. You'll need both for speech writing.

There are six sub-steps to this step to help you edit your document.

1. Edit for Focus: If there is something you wrote in the first draft that doesn't quite fit, change it. Be merciless in this step!

2. Edit for Clarity: Avoid tongue twisters, look for sentences that can be clearer, and get rid of any technical jargon.

3. Edit for Concision: Ask yourself if each piece of the presentation is essential. If it's not, get rid of it.

4. Edit for Continuity: Phrases, transition words, and sentences are all bridges to the next point in the

presentation. Be sure they're natural and feed into each other.

5. Edit for Variety: Never say the same words over and over again or you will lose the audience's attention.

6. Edit for Impact: Do you surprise the audience, make vivid images for them, appeal to their five senses, use memorable lines, use similes and analogies, and use rhetorical devices throughout the speech? Be sure you are.

Step Five – Apply Staging, Gestures, and Vocal Variety

Monotone delivery is going to put your audience to sleep, standing in one spot will do the same, and if you're not using staging, you're not entertaining. And a speech has to be entertaining on some level to keep the audience captivated, so this is just as important as your core point for your entire presentation. You can have an amazing core point, but if your presentation skills are lacking, then it's going to fall flat and the audience won't remember a thing.

Vocal Variety

A monotone delivery is going to have your audience snoring in no time. Follow the four P's to get an amazing speech with an amazing vocal delivery!

- Power: This is your volume. Your entire audience should be able to hear you without straining. In addition, turning your volume up and down will keep them from getting bored and they will continue to listen. Humans naturally listen to things that switch volume in order to figure out what it is. Eliminate outside noises if it's available to you. Use a microphone in large rooms.

- Pitch: Pitch is the frequency of sound you're speaking at. You're born with a voice pitch, but you can change your voice pitch to fit your speech. If you have characters in a speech, change your pitch to match their personality: higher for a child and lower for an adult male. It keeps the audience entertained and interested in the story.

- Pace: This is the rate at which you speak. Speed up to tell a dramatic story, slow down to deliver a key point or phrase. Varying your pace also keeps the audience listening.

- Pause: A short pause can signal the end of a sentence. A long pause can be between transitions or points. A pause before and after key points will buffer those points. Pauses after a rhetorical question make the audience think about the question and their answer. It keeps them on their toes.

Gestures

Gestures are very important when you're performing a speech, and they should seem as natural as possible. Be sure to practice them when you're practicing your speech so you get a flow going unique to you and conveys your message. Use these points to add gestures to your speech:

- Your body is going to naturally move as you speak, so let it. This expresses you're comfortable and confident when you're speaking.

- Mix in gestures with key points that are deliberate. Mimic the actions of the speech, like throwing a ball, or convey censorship by covering your mouth.

- Use a variety of gestures. Don't just get stuck with the same hand gesture over and over again.

- Don't forget about facial gestures! The audience is going to feed off your facial gestures, so smile at the right times and frown at other times.

Staging

Staging is imperative to your speech. The simplest part of staging is to prepare your speaking area before you actually start. Move obstacles out of your way and move the podium off to the side, or be aware of them. Be sure the people in the audience can clearly see you. Simple acts show the audience you've thought of them and you are prepared.

- If you use visual props or aids, plan where they're going to go before *and* after you use them. When they're not in use, they should be out of sight.

- Just as a pause can convey a transition, a movement can convey one, too.

- Map specific locations in the speaking area for certain stories. When you refer back to the story in the speech a second time, motion toward the area where you spoke to help them make a connection.

- In large rooms, balance your position on the left, right, and center of the area.

- Not every speech lets you do this, but move forward, backward, and up and down if you have the option.

Step Six – Practice and Self-Critique

Practicing your speech is going to be taken care of in the next chapter, but there are a few key points I want to mention.

- Recreate the speech setting by duplicating the surrounding area as much as you can.

  o Practice where you'll be giving the speech.

  o Stand up.

  o Use your props and visual aids.

  o Use an audience.

  o Consider what you're going to wear.

- Take notes and don't hesitate to jot down ideas in the middle of the rehearsal.

- Experiment with your gestures, voices, staging, and props to see what works best for you.

- Time yourself so you can insert some planned pauses and delays.

- Use all you learned to edit the speech and make it better. You're still not done writing it at this stage.

Once you've practiced alone, practice with an audience and get some feedback. Make sure you get constructive criticism and use an audience you can trust to give you an honest opinion.

Finally, after the speech is done and over with you want to self-critique yourself for the next speech. This is a learning process that will never end. You can always become a better speech giver, so always figure out what works best for you and try out new things, too.

Now you know how to write the speech and finish it, so let's talk more in depth about how you can practice at home.

Chapter Two – How to Practice Your Speech

Practicing your speech is essential to having a good speech, but practice is not going to make your speech perfect. What will make it perfect is revising and learning from your practices at home with or without an audience. There are many way you can practice a speech when you're at home, but let's first discuss what practicing is going to do for you.

So why should you practice a speech?

Practicing a speech is not going to make you perfect in any sense, but it is going to point out some things to you that will make your speech better.

- You'll be able to hear awkward expressions and tongue-twisters you may not have seen when you were writing and editing. Speaking the words out loud exposes those flaws, unlike reading or writing.

- You can gauge your energy level and adjust it so you're fired up in certain parts and a little more subdued in others. You can also determine if you're bored with the speech, which will definitely bore your audience.

- You can gauge your timing. Once you're experienced, you'll learn how many words are going to fit into a ten-minute time slot. Until then, you have to practice a complete speech to know if you're going to be under or over your time slot.

- Rehearsing is going to reduce your nervousness and improve your confidence in your material.

So how do you rehearse a speech at home?

Rehearsing just one time is going to improve your confidence in the speech you've written. You can practice for sixty hours or sixty minutes, but either way you should use some of these tips to make your speech the best it can be.

<u>Recreate the Setting</u>

Reading the speech at a computer screen is not going to make you feel more confident about your material. That is unless you're going to be doing a webcast. If that's the case, practice at the screen all you want! Otherwise, try to duplicate your setting like this:

- If you can book the room you'll be speaking in, then go for it and practice there! That's the best place to practice because you'll be able to hear yourself talking and hear your pitch, speed, and know how much room you have for gesturing.

- Stand up so you can hear your voice being projected. This gives you confidence and will tell you when to speak up or tone it down.

- Rehearse with your props and visual aids so you know where they're going to go after you're done with them. No one wants to trip over a visual aid while they're talking.

- Practice with an audience you know will give you feedback.

- Consider what you're going to wear. Will it create complications or will it inhibit your gestures? Make sure it's comfortable and you'll feel professional in it!

- Take notes as you practice so you know where to improve the second time you practice.

- Don't hesitate to stop in the middle of rehearsal and jot down some ideas. Capture those internal emotions immediately and figure out how you can express them to the audience or deal with them if it's stage fright.

Experiment

Don't be afraid to try out different gestures, voices, and staging. This is imperative for your introduction, conclusion, and key points throughout the speech.

Timing

Most speeches have to be delivered in a certain amount of time, so use a stopwatch or an app on your phone to time your speech and make sure it's within the amount you need.

Get Feedback

After the rehearsal, you want to actively ask members of the audience for some feedback. Did your humor get any laughs? Did you keep their attention throughout the speech? If you can't answer those questions, ask the audience. You can also ask them other things, such as:

- What was your favorite part and why?

- What would you want to see improved?

- How can the speech be improved for the next time?

This is much better than just asking if they liked it. It gives them the opportunity to be truly honest with you.

Use Audio Recordings

It might seem silly, but audio recordings of your speech are going to tell you your pace, pause, and pitch when you're delivering the speech. Assess phrases that sound good and ones that are awkward. Listen for any filler words like um and ah and notice if you stumble. Time the speech and individual components of the speech when you listen to it.

Video Recordings

A video recording is a very powerful tool. All your movements and habits are captured on film and you get to study them so you can change what you're doing on stage. You can look to see if:

- Your gestures work.

- The gestures are synchronized with words.

- The gestures are varied or all the same.

- Whether or not you're smiling.

- If you're fidgeting or using distracting motions.

- If you're swaying from nervousness.

Practicing at home with just a mirror is suitable, too because it will allow you to see what you're doing and let you hear yourself. Just remember to practice. Even just once can change your entire speech!

Chapter Three – Top Ten Mistakes to Avoid

I'm not telling you this to frighten you, but to educate you so you can have a much more professional presence on stage. These top ten mistakes should be considered as you are writing the speech and as you are practicing the speech. Be sure you're not doing any of these or you will lose your audience.

#1 Lazy Profanity

Profanity can be used in some speeches, and in some cases it's entertaining. If your audience is just some friends at a small, close wedding, profanity can be okay. If it's a business meeting, strangers, an educational speech, or anything professional in just the slightest, profanity is not okay. It's also not okay to use excessive profanity because people will begin to wonder if you don't know how to articulate using anything else. So keep profanity to a minimum when it comes to being with friends, and keep it out entirely when you're not in close company.

#2 Lateness

If you're late, you're insulting the audience. Even if it's a good excuse, you've still wasted their time. So do everything in your power to be at the venue where you will speak *early* so you don't have the opportunity to be late.

#3 Leering

It's awkward, but it's true. Men *and* women both leer at people they're attracted to, but when you're giving a professional speech, keep your eyes on nothing but other eyes. No up and down looks, especially onstage.

#4 Pollyannaish

The word translates to being overoptimistic. Take, for example, someone who has just experienced a natural disaster and nothing is okay at the moment, but they keep going and claim everything is okay right then. It kind of undermines their professionalism.

#5 Being Flighty

When it comes to doing a speech, let's say you promise to deliver an answer to a question in the introduction, and when you get the conclusion, the audience is wondering where the answer was. That's being a little flighty. They don't know the point of your speech then.

#6 Being Disorganized

If your speech is disorganized and you're trying to get a point across, people are going to wonder if you're really a reliable source. They're also going to wonder what the point was of sitting there listening to you talk. So you should be organized in every aspect of your speech.

#7 Inarticulateness

Have you ever been in a conversation with someone who used like all the time when it wasn't necessary or they rambled about something without really getting to the point? That's being inarticulate, and it can be very annoying for an audience. Get to the point and never use filler words such as like in your speech. You might be professional and well educated, but being inarticulate will make you come across as someone who's never stepped inside a school or learned any type of grammar.

#8 Secrecy

Speeches are meant to convey a message or a point, not to make the audience wonder about your personal life or your professional life. Don't be secretive in a business speech or the employees are going to think you're hiding something, well, because you probably are. Keep the secrecy out of the speech.

#9 Overpromising

The heart of selling to an audience is promising the maximum you can but being consistent with what you can actually deliver. Therefore, never promise an audience something you can't give them that very second. Someone might call you on it and you'll look bad, really bad.

#10 Cheating and Lying

Just like in a relationship, cheating and lying to your audience is not going to go over well. They trust you to tell them the facts and the truth. If you don't, everything you just told them is going to go out the window. They won't take away *any* points from your speech if you lie to them.

Now you know the top ten mistakes made by other speech writers and public speakers, so let's take a look at the more personal side of the process, overcoming stage fright.

Chapter Four - How to Overcome Stage Fright

If you're reading a book about public speaking, I'm going to assume you probably suffer from stage fright. It's not an uncommon occurrence, and many professional public speakers have admitted having stage fright over the years. If they can get up on a stage almost every day and make a living at giving speeches, despite suffering from stage fright, then you can move past it, too. I'm not going to say it is going to go away. It's more about changing your outlook and recognizing what is happening. Then you can move past it, but you might always have a little twinge before you go onstage to speak.

Remember Who Is Performing

Remember the audience is there to see you and hear you. It's your expertise, your gift to them, and your unique ability to get them out of their house and to their seat as your audience member. Of all the people in that room, you're the one who knows more about what is going to be said and who is going to be performing than anyone else there. Let yourself be the master of that moment.

Forget the Stakes

You heard me. Forget about who's in front of you for the time being. You've thought about that enough as you prepared, so take a good look at the people who are going to be listening to you and realize they are *just like you*. And you know what? They don't matter. You're the one performing.

Performance over the Audience

What you're delivering is actually more important than who you're delivering it to. Yes, the audience matters, but you've already factored that in. When it comes time to deliver the speech, you are the one who matters at that moment. Maintain your focus on your performing and not your audience. You should have practiced enough with a fake audience to know if they will like the jokes or not.

Be a Broadcaster

Radio and television are great proving grounds for actors and on stage performers because they allow you to practice without the physical distraction of having a visible audience. It sounds simplistic, but get some time with a camera and a microphone in order to focus more on the performance than the audience. Remember to practice so you can review yourself later and critique your movements.

Practice Like You Mean It

The worst mistake performers make is they do not feel the weight of the performance before they actually deliver it. If you don't perform at your full volume, pitch, and cadence, your body and mind are not going to know what it's going to be like and have the chance to adapt. So replicate your performance as much as you can before you actually do it.

Visualize Mistakes

There's always that moment when you realize you made a mistake onstage, so what are you going to do about it? It's best to visualize those mistakes before they ever happen so you can have a game plan. If they don't occur, great, if they do, no big deal; you have a plan for what you're going to do no matter what. If your worst fear is you're going to sneeze during your presentation, think about what you'll say and how you'll move on. If it's you'll show up with no pants on, then think about your preparation before the speech and how you can avoid that error.

Slow Down

When someone is nervous, they tend to speed up their speech so much the audience cannot keep up. This increases the likelihood of slipping up and saying something embarrassing or detrimental to the speech, so slow down. Use a metronome during rehearsal to control the speed at which you're talking. This forces your brain to get into a workable pace.

Buffer Your Performance

Arrive where you're going to speak early, and arrive alone or with a few supporters who understand you need some space. Settle in and disconnect from everyone around you. Turn the smartphone off. Use this time to review lines and notes, and have a beverage that's non-alcoholic and non-caffeinated to get in the mood. Over time, you'll have personal rituals that will help you get into the mindset of what you're about to do and what you want to achieve.

We'll talk more about how to take control of your thoughts and emotions before you get onstage and when you're actually on stage in chapter six. First, let's talk more about your body language.

Chapter Five – Using Body Language to Engage the Audience

Body language during a speech can actually convey more than your words do. Humans are very perceptive when it comes to body language, and they know when it's forced and when it's true. So use some of these techniques to be more aware of your posture, body movements, facial expressions, and eye contact throughout your speech.

Remove Noisy Movements

Remember how in chapter one you applied purposeful movements to your speech? Well, you can also apply noisy movement to your speech that don't really pertain to the speech. Movement that doesn't have a purpose is noisy movement.

For many, there is as much to be gained by getting rid of nervous and distracting movement and adding in purposeful gestures. Before you deliver a speech, ask someone while you're practicing what your most distracting physical movement or mannerism is. Everyone has one. Some people wring their hands, others play with coins in their pockets, while some will twirl their hair or bite their lips. It could be rocking back and forth from your heel to your toes, anything really.

Make a conscious effort to reduce or remove these from your speech entirely. By doing this, you clear the physical palette for purposeful gestures and movements that complement the speech instead of detract from it.

Avoid Forced Gestures

One common mistake many people see in speech givers is the project is overdone with awkward hand gestures in almost every sentence. This will result in a choppy and awkward delivery of the content.

Remember the goal is to not to provide the audience with an interpretation of every word spoken with a gesture. Instead, add gestures where they will have the most impact. The best way to avoid forcing hand and arm movements is to strike a balance between them and another physical gesture, like eye contact, facial expressions, and posture. If you convey an imperative emotion with facial expressions, the arms can relax because they are not needed at the time.

Record a Video of Yourself

If you have not looked at yourself performing your speech yet, use this moment to do it. The best way to discover if you have distracting gestures or movement is to watch yourself delivering the speech with the volume turned off. Take a look at the following points to watch out for:

- Does your body always move or are you coming to rest between gestures?

- Are your gestures conveying emotion without sound? Do they match the message?

- Is your face flat or expressive?

- Are your eyes darting around the room or are you maintaining gentle eye contact?

The best way to determine if you are creating enough movement but not distracting movement in a speech is to talk with an audience watching you or watch yourself on video to see what you might be doing wrong. Then come up with some alternative movements as solutions.

Next, we're going to talk about how to take control of those thoughts and emotions so you can deliver a powerful speech!

Chapter Six - Taking Control of Your Thoughts and Emotions

A commonly accepted definition of stress is when someone believes the demands of something exceed their social and personal resources they have access to. When people are stressed, they make two judgments. They feel threatened by the situation. And they feel they must judge whether or not their resources and capabilities are sufficient in order to meet that threat.

How stressed a person feels depends on how much damage they believe the situation will cause them. Perception is the key to making a situation not stressful anymore. It's your interpretation of the situation driving the stress levels you're feeling. Sometimes you are right in what you feel because some situations can be dangerous or threaten you physically, emotionally, or mentally. Stress is your early warning system that alerts you to a situation that threatens you.

However, sometimes you're harsh and unjust to yourself in a way you wouldn't be with a team member or a family member. Negative thinking coupled with this unfair judgment of yourself can cause stress to become severe and undermine your self-confidence.

Here are some tools you can use to overcome this stress before you begin a speech.

Thought Awareness

When you think negatively about the future and put yourself down, you damage your confidence and put your performance in jeopardy. A major problem with negative thoughts is they will flit into your consciousness, do their damage, and are gone in a second. Their significance has barely been noticed, and since you don't challenge them or correct them, you don't pay attention to them. That doesn't get rid of their harmful effects, though.

Thought awareness is the ability to observe your thought and become aware of *everything* that pops into your mind. One way to do this is to become more aware of your thoughts by streaming your consciousness when you think about a stressful situation. Don't suppress the thoughts, but let them run their course as you watch them and write them down as they happen.

Another general approach is to log stress in a diary. One of the benefits of doing this is, for one or two weeks, you will log all the unpleasant things that cause you stress in your life. This includes negative thoughts and anxieties, and can include memories or situations you perceive as being negative.

When you log these, you are able to find patterns in negative thinking. When you analyze the diary, you can see the most common and damaging thoughts you have. Tackle those as your priority first. Thought awareness is the first step to managing your negative thoughts. Without being aware of them, you have no idea how to control them.

Rational Thinking

The following step to deal with your negative thoughts is to challenge them with rational thinking. Look at every thought you wrote in that diary and challenge them by asking yourself whether they're reasonable and do they stand up to fair scrutiny.

Let's say you've had some of the following negative thoughts.

- You feel inadequate.

- You worry your performance will not be good enough.

- Anxiety that everything is out of your control undermines your efforts.

- You worry about how people will react to your work.

Now let's look at how you can challenge these thoughts.

- Feeling inadequate: Are you educated and have you trained for your speech? Do you have the resources you need to perform it well? Have you prepared and have you done all of this and still feel inadequate? Then maybe you're setting yourself too high of standards for this speech. Analyze and see if it's true.

- Worries about your performance: Do you have the training reasonable for this task? Have you planned? Have you prepared for this speech? If you haven't, then do those things. If you have, then know you are well positioned to give the best speech you can.

- Problems with issues outside of your control: Have you made a contingency plan for things that might go wrong? Did you think about the risks and challenges appropriately? If you can say yes, then you are well prepared to handle problems that may arise. If not, then write down your fears and go over what you can do to prevent them.

- Worry about other's reactions: If you put in the effort to prepare and you are doing the best you can, then that's all you need to know. If you perform as well as you possibly can, and you stay focused on your audience, then fair people are going to respond well. If people are not fair, it's not something you can control.

Positive Thinking and Opportunity Seeking

Where you use rational thinking to challenge those incorrect negative thinking, it's also useful to use positive, rational thoughts and affirmations that will counter them. It's also good to look at a situation and notice if there are opportunities offered by it.

Affirmations will help you build self-esteem and self-confidence. When you base your affirmations on clear, rational assessments of truths you made using the rational thinking section, you are able to undo the damage done by negative thinking.

Affirmations have to be strong and specific. They should be expressed in the current moment and have a very strong emotional content.

In addition to using affirmations, part of positive thinking is to look at opportunities the situation can offer you. If you successfully overcome the aforementioned obstacles in the last section, then the situation may offer you a positive opportunity. You might gain new skills, be seen as someone who handles difficult tasks, and open up new career opportunities.

Be sure to take the time to identify those opportunities and focus on them when you think positive.

Now you know how to get past emotionally negative thoughts and take control of your thought process, so let's take a look at how you can really grab the audience for an amazing public speech!

Chapter Seven – Proven Ways to Grab the Audiences' Attention

If you have been waiting for the moment I tell you how to make your speech more than just good, but amazing, then this is that moment. In this chapter, I'm going to tell you how you can grab ahold of the audience verbally and keep them enraptured with your words. It's all about their emotions and how they're interpreting what you're saying, and you can really keep them engaged with a few simple tricks.

#1 Give Them Something to Take Home

Provide something specific for the audience to take home with them. It doesn't matter how inspiring your message is, every audience wants to learn a tangible way they can apply what they've learned to their lives this moment. So don't be afraid to tell them to do something that night, right away, and then tell them how they can fix it tomorrow.

#2 Don't Defer Questions

If someone has a question in the middle of a presentation, that's an amazing thing! Someone is actually listening to what you're saying! Seize that opportunity and address their question, even if it's further along in the presentation. Practice skipping around so you can do this if a question comes up. The best presentation is going to feel like a conversation, even if that conversation is one-sided. So don't ever ignore someone's question.

#3 Ask Questions You Can't Answer

When you ask a question to engage your audience it usually feels forced. Instead, ask a question you know they can't answer and tell them it's okay, you can't answer that question either. Explain why you're not able to answer that question and then talk about what you do know about the topic at hand. Most speakers tell you they have all the answers, but if you tell the audience you don't and you're willing to admit that honestly, then that humanizes you and make the audience pay attention to what you do know.

#4 Fuel Your Mental Engine

Did you know dopamine and epinephrine help regulate your mental alertness? Both of them come from tyrosine which is an amino acid found in protein. Therefore include protein in the meal before you do your speech. Don't wait until the last second because the last thing you're going to want to do is eat before a public speech.

#5 Burn off Some Cortisol

This is dispersed by your adrenal glands when you're feeling stressed or anxious. High levels can limit originality and the capability to process information, and when you're high on cortisol, it's almost unmanageable to react to your audience and read them. The easiest way to burn that off is to exercise. Work out before you go to work, take a walk at lunch, or hit the gym before you go to a speaking engagement.

#6 Make Contingency Plans

I don't think I can mention this enough. Come up with all the 'what ifs' you can and answer them. Such as, what if there's a fire during your speech? What if someone asks a question you can't answer? What if you suddenly lose your voice? All of those are things you should think about and try to come up with what you might do. Odds are none of those things are going to happen, but thinking about what you'll do in that situation and having a plan for it will make you feel more confident while you're on stage. You'll have a clear idea of what you'd do in a 'what if' situation.

#7 Make a Pre-Routine

Instead of having superstitions like a lucky pair of socks or a lucky bracelet, make a routine that allows you to center yourself emotionally. Walk into the room you'll perform in ahead of time to check sight lines. Check the microphones and go through your presentation at the sight before it's time to do the speech.

#8 Set a Backup Goal

What if you're speaking to a charity and your presentation starts to fall flat? In response, people will try too hard or give up. If your goal is to land a contract and you believe you won't succeed, shift to trying to plant the seeds for a future speech down the road. If you see you won't get what you want right away, why can't you make room to try again in the future?

#9 Share an Emotional Story

We all have ones. Everyone has a moment in their life that was really emotional for them, and you don't necessarily have to use yours. Tell a story that will capture the audience and be emotional about it. If you feel sad, show it and tell them how you felt. If you felt angry or hurt, tell them. If you cried, tell them. When you share your true feelings about a story, you create a lasting connection with your audience.

#10 Pause for Ten Seconds

Pause for just three seconds and the audience thinks you lost your place. Five seconds and they believe it's an intentional pause. Ten seconds and the ones who got lost or started texting are now looking up. When you start to speak again, they assume the pause was deliberate and you are a poised speaker. A poor speaker will abhor a vacuum, only self-assured speakers are confident with their silence. Take a long pause to gather your thoughts and the audience gives you speaker bonus points.

#11 Share Something They Don't Know

No one ever says something about the fancy chart you put on the screen, but if you tell them their stomach lining blushes when their face blushes, they won't forget it anytime soon. Find something fun, interesting, and different to share with them and they will immediately start paying attention.

#12 Benefit the Audience

Stop thinking about sales and start thinking about what you can tell the audience that will benefit them. Put your focus on being sure the audience will benefit from what you say and they will automatically listen.

#13 Don't Make Excuses

Don't tell an audience you're not good at something or you didn't have enough time to prepare. They will automatically get angry that you're wasting their time. Just go ahead and do it, and forget about the excuses.

#14 Don't Do Prep Onstage

Do not wait until you're on the stage to check lighting, the mic, the remote, or the presentation. Do all of that before the audience fills in so you look set up and ready to go. If there are people who run those functions, talk to them to see what can be done if something goes wrong. And if something does go wrong, smile and look confident while you or someone else takes care of the problem. Your reaction is the most important part of whether or not something goes wrong.

#15 Don't Overload Slides

Make sure the font size is double the average age of the audience. So the font should be between sixty and eighty in size. If you need to fit more words on, then you haven't tightened the message.

#16 Don't Read Slides

The audience should be able to scan the slide, not have to read the slide. If they do, you'll lose them. And if you read them, you'll most definitely lose them. The slide is the accent point, not the actual point.

#17 Focus on Attention

Instead of telling people to turn off their cell phones and making yourself look like their teacher and not an equal, focus on earning their attention. That's right, earn it. Make the presentation so interesting and entertaining they won't want to look at their phones. It's not their job to listen to you, it's your job to make them want to listen.

#18 Repeat Audience Questions

Unless a microphone is being used, it's unlikely everyone in the audience heard the question another audience member asked. Repeat the question and then answer it so people know what you're talking about. It's courteous and provides you with some time to think of a great way to answer the question.

#19 Repeat Yourself

The audience is going to hear about half of what you say, and then they're going to filter in with their own perspectives. Create a structure that lets you repeat and reinforce your key points. First explain the point, and then give some examples of how it can be applied and at the end the audience has action steps to take home.

#20 Run Short

If you have thirty minutes, then take twenty-five. If you have an hour, take fifty minutes. Always respect the time of your audience and end a little early. As a bonus, you hone your presentation and can shift gears if the presentation takes an unexpected turn. Finish early and ask for questions. Invite them to see you after the presentation. Never run long because all you just told them will most likely be forgotten.

And that's how you make an amazing presentation!

Conclusion

Public speaking can be nerve-wracking and downright terrifying if you're not prepared, but if you did all of the things I told you to in this book, you will have an excellent speech. Remember you are not standing up there for just you, but you're standing up there to speak to an audience that should want to hear what you're saying. Always be sure you're not bored with what you're writing or speaking, that way you will be engaged so the audience will follow.

Giving a speech does not have to be a frightening, terrifying ordeal. The only person who makes it this way is you, so use some of the suggestions in chapter six to take control of those thoughts and emotions, and make your speech shine. Grab your audience with one of the many ways to get their attention in chapter seven, and most importantly, have fun! Speeches are about conveying information in a way that helps the audience connect with the speaker. Treat these people with respect but as your equals, and you will have earned their attention.

I hope you enjoyed the tips you found in this eBook on public speaking. If so, please leave a review at your online eBook retailer's website.

Thank you for reading!

-- Neal Hoffman

Check Out Other Books

Seven Everyday Anti-Aging Habits: Daily practices to help you look younger, slimmer and happier.

http://www.amazon.com/Seven-Everyday-Anti-Aging-Habits-practices-ebook/dp/B00RRBZLPO

How to Enjoy After Retirement: Ultimate Guide to stay Healthy, Happy and Financially Independent.

http://www.amazon.com/How-Enjoy-After-Retirement-Financially-ebook/dp/B00UBC3YT6

Simplify Your Lifestyle: Seven Steps To A Clutter Free Home and Happy Living with Less.

http://www.amazon.com/Simplify-Your-Lifestyle-Clutter-Living-ebook/dp/B00VZ0YOWO

How To Practice Mindfulness: Step-by-Step Techniques For Beginners.

http://www.amazon.com/How-Practice-Mindfulness-Step---Step-ebook/dp/B00Z4C31CS

www.ingramcontent.com/pod-product-compliance
Lightning Source LLC
Chambersburg PA
CBHW070924180526
45168CB00005B/2136